fP

ALSO BY JUDITH VIORST

POEMS

The Village Square

It's Hard to Be Hip Over Thirty and Other Tragedies of Married Life

People and Other Aggravations

How Did I Get to Be Forty and Other Atrocities

If I Were in Charge of the World and Other Worries

When Did I Stop Being Twenty and Other Injustices

Forever Fifty and Other Negotiations

Sad Underwear and Other Complications

Suddenly Sixty and Other Shocks of Later Life

CHILDREN'S BOOKS

Sunday Morning

I'll Fix Anthony

Try It Again, Sam

The Tenth Good Thing About Barney

Alexander and the Terrible, Horrible, No Good, Very Bad Day

My Mama Says There Aren't Any Zombies, Ghosts, Vampires, Creatures, Demons, Monsters, Fiends, Goblins, or Things

Rosie and Michael

Alexander, Who Used to Be Rich Last Sunday

The Good-bye Book

Earrings!

The Alphabet From Z to A (With Much Confusion on the Way)

Alexander, Who's Not (Do You Hear Me? I Mean It!) Going to Move

Absolutely Positively Alexander

Super-Completely and Totally the Messiest

OTHER

Yes, Married

A Visit From St. Nicholas (To a Liberated Household)

Love & Guilt & the Meaning of Life, Etc.

Necessary Losses

Murdering Mr. Monti

Imperfect Control

You're Officially a Grown-Up

Grown-Up Marriage

I'm Too Young to Be Seventy

And Other Delusions

JUDITH VIORST

Illustrated by Laura Gibson

Free Press
NEW YORK   LONDON   TORONTO   SYDNEY

FREE PRESS
A Division of Simon & Schuster, Inc.
1230 Avenue of the Americas
New York, NY 10020

Text copyright ©2005 by Judith Viorst
Illustrations copyright ©2005 by Laura Gibson

FREE PRESS and colophon are
trademarks of Simon & Schuster, Inc.

For information about special discounts for bulk purchases, please contact
Simon & Schuster Special Sales:
1-800-456-6798 or business@simonandschuster.com

Designed by Karolina Harris

Manufactured in the United States of America

1   3   5   7   9   10   8   6   4   2

Library of Congress Cataloging-in-Publication Data
Viorst, Judith.
I'm too young to be seventy: and other delusions / Judith Viorst; illustrated by Laura Gibson.
p. cm.
1. Humorous poetry, American. 2. Marriage—Poetry. 3. Family—Poetry. 4. Aging—Poetry.
I. Title.
PS3572.I6 I47   2005
811'.54—dc22   2005047706

ISBN-13: 978-0-7432-6774-8
ISBN-10:   0-7432-6774-5

for
Joan and Leonard Beerman
Lisbeth and Daniel Schorr
and in memory of
Grace and Harold Willens

Contents

The Rest of It

At Seventy

At Seventy

Instead of "old,"
Let us consider
"Older,"
Or maybe "oldish,"
Or something, anything,
That isn't always dressed
In sensible shoes
And fading underwear.
Besides which,
Seventy isn't old.
Ninety is old.
And though eighty
Is probably old,
We needn't decide that
Until we get there.
In the meantime
Let us consider
Drinking wine,
Making love,
Laughing hard,
Caring hard,
And learning a new trick or two
As part of our job description
At seventy.

Erotic Options

I've never greeted my husband at the door
Naked except for a necklace and high-heeled shoes.
I've never, when offered adulterous amour,
Found it especially difficult to refuse.

I've never made mad love on my kitchen floor,
Or slept with some nameless stranger on a cruise.
I've never considered having any more
Than a total of two in bed. How would I choose?

I've never attempted anything hard core
With ice cubes, or whips, or cranberry-orange juice.
I've never played Teacher or Nurse or Belle de Jour,
Or pursued a Havana cigar's alternative use.

I've never felt strongly prompted to explore
Other erotic options. A monkey? A moose?
But if, in my eighties, sex starts becoming a bore,
I fully intend to consider letting loose.

Teeth

Though I brush twice a day and am deeply committed to flossing,
I'm finding that I, and that most of the people I know,
Now require not only a regular family dentist,
But also two dontists—one endo and one perio.
At costs far surpassing our annual mortgage payments,
In states of mind ranging from panic to weak in the knees,
I've acquired a mouthful of crowns, veneers, bridges, and
    implants,
So I'll be at my best when photographers tell me, "Say cheese."

I'm smiling a strong, sturdy smile because my retainer
Discourages slipping and grinding when popped in at night.
And I'm smiling a radiant smile because of those treatments
That bleach out the yellow and leave me with Tom-Cruise-ish
    white.
And I'm smiling a gapless smile because I've had bonding
To close up those spaces in which spinach used to repose.
And I'm smiling a confident smile because, at the moment,
I'm sure nothing awful is going on under my nose.

And yet, when I think of the drill, the novocaine needles,
Those sharp metal instruments Human Rights Watchers should
    ban,
When I think about having to open wider and wider
And how I feel worse when I'm finished than when I began,
And when I consider my grandchildren's college tuitions,
And the fortune in dentists and dontists I cannot bequeath,
I wonder if maybe I should have at least considered
A water glass and a set of removable teeth.

Hmmm

The coward dies a thousand deaths,
The brave but one,
I try telling myself
When my doctor says, "Hmmm,"
Instead of saying,
"Everything looks fine,"
And orders more tests.

And while I am waiting,
And dying one of my thousand deaths,
Of whatever it is I'm being tested for,
I try telling myself
That I've had a good life,
That my children are grown and don't need me so much anymore,
And that since this could be my last March 18th
Or August 24th,
I ought to try to savor every second.

And while I am waiting,
And dying one of my thousand deaths,
And keeping in mind my good life
And my grown children,
And working on savoring every single second,
I am telling myself
To try to act plucky and spunky as well as inwardly serene,
Which is how, when I'm gone,
I'd like to be remembered.

And while I am waiting,
And dying one of my thousand deaths,
And keeping in mind my good life
And my grown children,
And working on savoring every goddamn second,
And knocking my brains out acting as if
I'm plucky and spunky and inwardly serene,
My doctor calls to tell me that I passed the tests and
Everything looks fine.

Deaths died: One.
Deaths left: Nine hundred and ninety-nine.

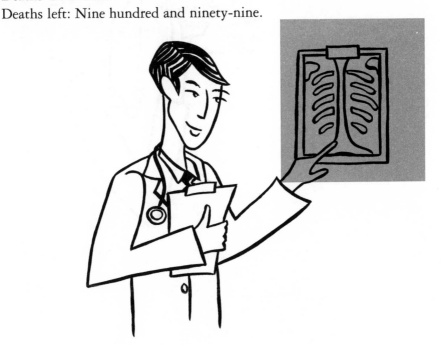

Re: Vision

No lines on my face.
No gray in my hair.
No stains on my clothes where I spilled
In the course of one of my fork-to-mouth
Incomplete passes.
No dust on the tables.
No spots on the rugs.
I'm absolutely thrilled
At how perfect the world becomes
When I take off my glasses.

As Time Goes By

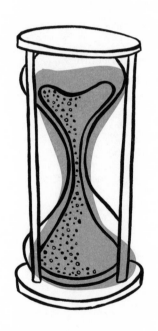

I wake up on Monday,
Eat lunch on Wednesday,
Go to sleep on Friday,
And next thing I know it's
The middle of next week
And I am shaking mothballs
Out of the winter clothes
I stored for the summer
Five minutes ago,
Because snowstorms follow
The Fourth of July
Faster than faxes,
Faster than e-mail,
Faster, maybe, than the speed of light.

You want to slow down time?
Try root canal.
Try an MRI.
Try waiting for the report on the biopsy.
Or try being a child on a rainy morning
With nothing to do,
Wishing away the hours, the days, the years,
As if there will
Always
Always
Always
Be more.

Soul-Searching

Am I required to think of myself as a basically shallow woman
Because I feel better when my hair looks good?
Does knowing that it's an absolutely stupid superstition
Mean that I have to give up knocking wood?
Is it okay to be someone who's both attuned to the woes of the
    world,
And likes to shop?

How long, if I don't succeed, do I need to keep trying and trying
 and trying
Before I can stop?
Couldn't it just be possible that by never flying on planes
I could remain indefinitely alive?
How much do I love my family if, when everyone comes for
 Thanksgiving,
I'm almost as glad when they leave as when they arrive?
How much do I love my grandkids if, when I'm wearing my
 beige silk suit,
I won't let them hug me unless their hands are clean?
Am I a serious person if, along with Leo Tolstoy and Emily
 Dickinson,
I also like reading *People* magazine?
Isn't it time to accept that no matter how rigorously I exercise,
My body is best seen covered rather than bare?
Why am I still expecting that a handsome stranger, some
 enchanted evening,
Will rush to my side and want to start an affair?
When do I acquire that seasoned perspective, that sense of
 proportion, that quiet composure
That will keep me from going berserk when I misplace my keys?
And how old do I have to be before I finally can allow myself
To do exactly—exactly!—what I damn please?

Still
Married

The Secret
of Staying Married

Still married after all these years?
No mystery.
We are each other's habit,
And each other's history.

Not Merely
His Life Companion

I swear that he drove through a red—not a yellow—light,
Plus he's doing 61 in a 50-mile zone,
And he's in the wrong lane if he plans to take a right.
I mention all this in a loving, respectful tone,
While alerting him to the fellow crossing the street,
And the fact that he's way too close to the car ahead.
I speak in a voice so gentle, so soft, and so sweet
That he really should be ashamed of what he just said.
But as undeterred by his words as I've always been,
I suggest putting on the brights because of the snow,
Observe that he almost collided when he cut in,
And point out that a stop sign means stop—full stop—not slow,
And that if he makes that U-turn we'll probably die.
But I never convey either rancor or reproach,
Hoping that one of these years he'll be grateful that I
Am not merely his life companion but driving coach.

Body Heat

Over the decades we finally worked out
How much is enough insurance,
How long should his mother visit,
How many times a week is plenty of sex,
But lately I'm in the kitchen with my sweater and fleece-lined
    jacket and oven on,
(Despite which I'm so cold I could freeze to death like an Eskimo
    left out on an ice floe),
While he's sitting there at the table in a short-sleeved shirt and
    bare feet,
Asking could I at least crack open the door,
And maybe we'll have to start eating in separate rooms for the
    rest of our lives,
Since we've become thermostatically incompatible.

Over the decades we finally worked out
That camping is not a vacation,
That valet parking is not a self-indulgence,
That a husband could love you and still leave the toilet seat up,
But lately I'm lying in bed, and I'm naked and moaning and
    sweating and flushed and gasping for breath,
(Not out of passion but only because I'm so hot I will probably
    die from heat prostration),
While he's lying right beside me under two blankets and a pair of
    flannel pajamas,

Asking could I at least keep the window closed,
And maybe we'll have to start sleeping in separate rooms for the
    rest of our lives,
Since we've become thermostatically incompatible.

Over the decades we finally worked out
When it's time to go home from the party,
When it's grubby rather than charming,
When you don't help yourself to the food off your spouse's plate,
But lately I'm cold when he's hot and I'm hot when he's cold and
    between the two of us
Are sixty-five degrees of separation,
And we haven't worked out how we're going to live together the
    rest of our lives,
Since we've become thermostatically incompatible.

Why Marriage Was Invented

We're on our way to the party, our speed decreased
Because we can't remember our hostess's name.
I say it has three syllables at least.
He says it's like a boy's, but not the same.

I say it rhymes with "skirt" and starts with "R."
He says it ends with "a" and not with "t."
And just before we've finally parked the car,
We reach "Roberta" simultaneously.

In our long years together we have shared
One family and one life of joy and pain,
Not knowing that we've slowly been prepared
To—fifty/fifty—also share one brain.

At the Opera

My husband sits beside me at the opera,
Sighing heavily,
And making it clear
As he tap-tap-taps the armrest with one finger
And crosses, uncrosses, recrosses his navy blue legs,
That although Don Giovanni will eventually wind up in Hell,
He—my husband—is already there.

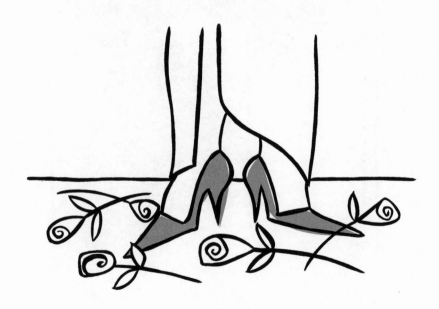

While everyone else is shouting "bravo" or "brava" at the end of
  each aria,
And leaping to their feet to offer a standing ovation when the last
  curtain falls,
My husband is applauding sparsely, grudgingly, his sighs often
  louder than his applause,
Because he'd prefer to be taking the car for inspection,
Because he'd prefer to be caught in rush-hour traffic,
Because he'd prefer to be having a prostate exam.

He is not a whole lot of fun to bring to the opera.

Not to mention that I am expected, for each opera that he
  attends,
To spend an equivalent evening sitting beside him
Listening to a lecture on Gulf Security in Bahrain or someplace
  like Bahrain,
Which I have nothing against
Except I'd prefer to be doing our tax returns,
Except I'd prefer to be caught in rush-hour traffic,
Except I'd prefer to be having a mammogram.

Defiant and uncompromising,
The Don has gone to his death.
Undefiant and compromising,
My husband and I go home.
Tomorrow: Bahrain.

In the Middle
of the Night

In the middle of the night, while my husband is sleeping,
And I'm extremely awake in our double bed,
Worried about some meteorite that might smash into the Earth
And other matters inspiring major dread,
My husband, immune to anxiety, keeps sleeping.

Although I give him a sharp little poke with my elbow,
And yank both his pillows out from under his head,
And knee him, not especially gently, in the small of his back,
My husband isn't hearing a word I've said,
When I whisper in his good ear, "Are you still sleeping?"

Forget for better or worse and for richer or poorer.
Forget in sickness and health. One reason to wed
Is to have someone to hold hands with in the middle of the night,
Worrying about meteorites. Instead,
I worry alone while my husband goes on sleeping.

Up with his callous behavior I'm tired of putting.
Up with his insensitivity I am fed.
But up, though I've pulled his blanket off, he is refusing to be.
He sleeps the sleep of the dead. Could he be dead?
I turn on the light. Check his pulse. No, he's just sleeping.

Some of the Reasons I Love to Go to the Movies

I like strolls, not hikes,
Cars, not bikes,
Terraces, not peaks,
Swimming pools, not creeks,
And watching the sun set over the mountains
In streaks of red-gold splendor,
But only from picture windows, not from a tent.
Even for red-gold splendor
I do not do tents.

Nor do I do,
Despite some pressure from my husband,
Rushing off to meadows at five in the morning
To identify birds in their natural habitat,
Or bouncing along on African safaris
To gape at wild beasts in their natural habitat,
Or slogging my way through Amazonian jungles
To trip over vines in their natural habitat,
When home in my bed with my quilt and my special pillow
Happens to be my natural habitat.

I like it like that.
In addition to which
I like dry, not wet,
Perfume, not sweat,

Room service, not canteens,
Jacuzzis, not latrines,
And walking on beaches in late September,
A breeze gently blowing my hair,
But only before, not after, I've had my hair done.
Even for gentle breezes
I do not do after.

Nor do I do,
Despite some pressure from my husband,
Anything that might involve
Being bitten by mosquitoes,
Being sunk in mud up to my knees,
Being swept from canoes into churning rapids,
Being required to wear a pair of skis,
Or being asked to admire the view from the edge of a world-
    famous canyon
Where one false move and you plunge to your death below,
None of which could happen to me,
It's comforting to know,
When I go to the movies.

To My Husband When He Starts Contemplating Remarriage

or

If I Should Die Before I Wake, Here's the Wife You Next Should Take

Let her be loving and gentle and easy to be with.
Let her have great mental health, also trust funds galore.
Let her hold views that you practically always agree with.
Let her be so damn good-natured she's almost a bore.

Let her be younger than I am, but not what's called pretty.
Let her be only okay playing Scrabble and chess.
Let her do tax returns better than she can do witty.
Let her enjoy football plenty, and sex a lot less.

Let her be friends with the grandkids, but never their nana.
Let her provide dust-free baseboards and Internet skills.
Let her be more like Elizabeth than like Diana.
Let her strong suit be serenity rather than thrills.

Let her—of course!—bring some happiness into your life, dear.
Let her attend to your needs without making a fuss.
And each time you're asked to compare her with your late wife,
    dear,
Let her receive a B-minus, and me an A-plus.

The Children and Grandchildren

They May Be Middle Aged, But They're Still My Children

They may be middle aged,
But they're still my children,
And even though they think they don't need my advice,
They need it,
Because who else is going to tell them:
Check your moles once a year with the dermatologist,
Order the mixed green salad instead of the fries,
Peeing before a long car trip is always wise,
And call your Aunt Rhoda—a phone call wouldn't kill you.

They may be middle aged,
But I'm still their mother,
And even though they don't want me to give them advice,
I'm giving it,
Because who else is going to tell them:
Periodontal disease is no laughing matter,
Wipe between your toes when you're drying your feet,
Fasten your seat belt even in the backseat,
And shave off the mustache—it makes you look like Hitler.

They may be middle aged,
But they still could listen
When I tell them which neighborhoods aren't so safe to live in,
When I tell them that cabbage often causes gas,
When I tell them that when they serve cocktails outdoors, it's
   best to use plastic, not glass,
When I tell them that e-mail thank-you notes aren't thank-you
   notes,
When I tell them it never hurts to pay a compliment,
When I tell them that tax-free bonds are the way to go,
And when I tell them that even though
They may be middle aged,
They're my children.
They're still my children.
And I'm still their mother.

Granddaughter

for Olivia

How can a person not yet three years old
Already know that blue is her favorite color,
And hold fierce opinions on hairstyles and dress-up clothes,
And master the art of extracting one more candy bar and two
    more videos
From her spineless grandma?

Where does a person not quite three feet tall
Learn the strategic uses of smiles, sighs, and kisses,
And acquire a litigator's implacable skill,
Sufficient—in the case of child versus designated bedtime—to
    crush the will
Of her wimpy grandma?

Why is a person a mere thirty pounds
Mighty enough to disrupt an entire household,
Charming enough to persuade us to welcome the mess,
And persistent enough to convert a firm "no—and that's final!"
    into a "yes"
From her weak-minded grandma?

What makes a person so new to this world
So certain that I am her loyal and faithful servant,
Here to read books and to not feed her anything green,
While she, the kid in the training pants with the chocolate
    smudge on her cheek, is the absolute queen
Of her weak-minded, wimpy, spineless, besotted grandma?

New Kid
Around the House

for Nathaniel and Benjamin

My grandson, now a big brother, has decided
That there are a few benefits
To having a new kid around the house,
A new kid
Whose cries are loud,
Whose smells are stinky,
Whose sleeping habits are deplorable,
Who can't answer questions, wave bye-bye, or play hide-and-seek,
Who possesses, in fact, no discernible skills.
"Let's keep him," says my grandson, the big brother,
Offering him a stuffed panda losing its stuffing,
And smiling, as the new kid nuzzles his mother's brimming
    breast,
A smile of been-there-done-that superiority.

My grandson, now older and wiser, has decided
That there are few benefits
To having a new kid around the house,
A new kid
Whose cries are loud,
Whose smells are stinky,
Whose sleeping habits are deplorable,
Who can't answer questions, wave bye-bye, or play hide-and-seek,
But who nevertheless gets all the attention and breasts.
"Let's find his mother and give him back," says my grandson,
Retrieving the stuffed panda losing its stuffing,
And reproaching me, as I kiss the new kid and murmur,
"Aren't you sweet" and "You're just the cutest,"
With a glance I can only translate as "You too, Brutus?"

Namesakes

for Miranda and Brandeis

Our oldest son,
Working as a public defender,
Named his first child Miranda
And his second Brandeis.
It seemed, as they say,
Like a good idea at the time.
But now that Miranda has become
A preteen,
She insists on her right to remain silent,
While her brother Brandeis
Is a lad of many injudicious decisions,
None of which he expects
To have overruled.

A Letter to My Sons
About Mother's Day

Unlike King Lear, I am well aware
That extravagant expressions of affection
Do not necessarily mean that our children adore us,
Or that their failure to write or phone or do lots of lovely things
    for us
Means that they don't.
I am, in addition, well aware
That most of the wise, mature, sensible women I know
Have nothing but disdain for Mother's Day,
Which they rightfully declare to be a crass, commercial way
Of getting guilty children to spend money.
Furthermore, I am hoping that I
Will turn into one of those wise, mature, sensible women
Long before this current decade is through.
But meanwhile, if you know what's good for you,
Send flowers.

What Do We Tell the Children?

remembering 9/11

If we can't promise
That it will never happen again,
Or that it won't, if it happens again,
Happen to them,
Or if it does happen again,
And this time to them,
We will come save them,
Or that, if we can't save them,
Somebody else will,
Or that, if no one can save them,
It won't hurt,
Or it won't hurt that much,
Or it won't hurt that long,
Could we tell them
To please stop asking so many questions?

Role Reversal

Our children, with a touch of pique,
Complain we're out four nights a week,
And pressingly suggest we do more resting.
They offer us some dull advice
About the virtues of brown rice
And other foods we don't think worth ingesting.

They're urging us to sign up for
Some nice safe undemanding tour
In lieu of a far jauntier vacation,
And watch us disapprovingly
Drink every drop of our Chablis
Untroubled by their pleas for moderation.

They warn us we are sure to slip
And give ourselves a fractured hip
Unless, when climbing stairs, we grip the railing.
They tell us to slow down, relax,
Lift nothing that will strain our backs,
And take a pill for everything that's ailing.

We don't ail all that much. In fact,
We see ourselves as quite intact,
Despite some losses physical and mental.
So though we know no harm is meant,
We've come to mightily resent
Our children's tendency to act parental.

The Sixth Grandchild

for Isaac

Our number six has arrived,
The last but not least.
How our happiness has increased since he made
   his debut.
How our family has increased. We used to be two
And now we set the table for fourteen.
Who knew, on that long-ago night when we first danced
   to "Begin the Beguine,"
What we were beginning!

The Rest of It

Nervous

Athens Mayor Dora Bakoyannis, in charge of preparations for the Summer Olympics, says she is "paid to be nervous."
—THE WASHINGTON POST, JUNE 9, 2004

Nobody has to pay me to be nervous.
I've always done it as a volunteer.
I do it as a kind of public service
That draws upon my expertise in fear.

While some folks see a brighter day tomorrow,
I'm figuring it's wiser to beware,
And by anticipating future sorrow,
I prod the more insouciant to prepare.

I'm told that I get nervous prematurely
When what I ought to do is watch and wait.
But I say "better safe than sorry" surely
Protects us from "too little and too late."

I'm asked to make an effort to be jolly.
I quietly reply to this request
That circumstances soon will prove the folly
Of those who keep on hoping for the best.

Although Cassandras hold a lowly status,
The world needs someone to expect the worst.
And so I'm nervous, constantly and gratis,
Not ever to be thanked—or reimbursed.

Too Young to Be Seventy

Deep in my heart I believe I'm
Too young to be seventy.
There are times when I'm wearing my baseball cap and my jeans
That I even can imagine that, glimpsed from the rear, I might be
    mistaken
For someone who could still be in her teens.
Or maybe the mother of teens.
Late thirties?
Early forties?
Middle fifties?
I think I could do the middle fifties just fine,
Like that actress who, when asked how she could be fifty-four
    when her son was forty-eight,
Replied, "My son lives his life, and I live mine."

In the life that I'm living I'm
Too young to be seventy.
The woman I see in the mirror is not the real me.
When I elevate my chin,
When I suck my stomach in,
When I throw my shoulders back,
When I tighten all that's slack,
I can't be any more than
Sixty-one.
And a half?
Sixty-two?
Okay, sixty-three.

As long as we can agree I'm
Too young to be seventy.
Too young in my heart and my soul,
If not in my thighs.
Too hopeful.
Too eager.
Too playful.
Too restless.
Too insufficiently wise.
Too young.
Did I mention too young?
Too young to be seventy.

Keynesian Economics

Men do not realize how great an income thrift is.

—CICERO

I bought the generic gray slacks and not the designer ones. (Saved
$300.)
Plus a suit that was on a forty-percent-off sale. (Saved $280.)
I walked away from a scarf that would have looked perfect with
the suit,
Because the price was a little beyond the pale. (Saved $200.)
I also returned a jacket that didn't quite fit right,
Although it would have gone great with my new slacks. (Saved
$320.)
And I figure that I made, in a couple of hours,
Eleven hundred dollars shopping at Saks.

If We Stopped Trying

Though we tread the treadmill daily,
Give equal time to yoga and Pilates,
Pump iron, do our crunches, do our squats,
We are flabby of abs and of glutes.
Yet we stick to our sweaty pursuits because
Our bodies would be even flabbier
If we stopped trying.

Though we're members of a book club,
Take seminars on Keats and chaos theory,
Play tapes explaining lieder, Jung, and Chi,
We can barely remember a word.
Yet we're plugging away undeterred because
Our minds would be even fuzzier
If we stopped trying.

Though we march in demonstrations,
Write checks to fight injustice and diseases,
Defend the wetlands, ozone layer, and whales,
The whole world's in a terrible mess.
Yet we persevere nevertheless because
We can't let it get any worse,
And the world would become even worse,
The world would be a lot worse
If we stopped trying.

On Not Being a Good Sport About the Fact That I'm Going to Die One of These Days

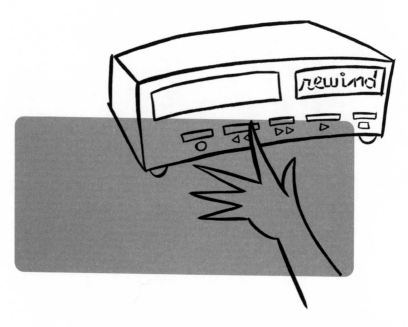

Unlike the seasons, no springtime will follow my winter.
Unlike a clock, my twelve midnight won't tick-tock toward one.
The wind's at my back and it's turning me into a sprinter,
Rushing along on a journey that's soon to be done.

Unlike a book, I can't start again from the beginning.
Unlike a video movie, I cannot re-wind.
The ice that is under my feet keeps on thinning and thinning.
Do I mind? Do I *mind?* You bet your sweet ass I mind.

At the Airport

The only thing worse than flying is missing the plane.

—OVERHEARD AT DULLES AIRPORT

I am sitting here at the airport
Two hours before my plane is due to depart,
Having checked my luggage,
Received my boarding pass,
And gone through Security.

There is a smile on my face,
And peace in my soul,
For I am soothed by the knowledge
That I am here, right here, in the departure area,
Not screaming at my husband that if we do not leave this second
    I'm leaving without him,
Not muttering, as our taxi is trapped in bumper-to-bumper
    traffic, that I said this would happen,
Not waiting in a line that extends from the X-ray machine out
    the door and onto the sidewalk,
Not racing back to Security to pick up the scarf and umbrella I
    left behind,
And not racing through the terminal from Gate 1 to Gate 59,
Hoping, as my heart starts pounding harder and harder and harder,
    that someone nearby will know how to use the defibrillator.

Let others seek inner peace in places of worship.
This is what I need to feel serene:
My boarding pass, a paperback book, a Starbucks cappuccino, a
    few magazines,
And me sitting here at the airport,
Sitting right here at the airport,
Sitting right here at the airport with this quiet smile on my face,
Two hours before my plane is due to depart.

Still Dieting
After All These Years

So perhaps when I am *eighty*,
I won't care about my weight. E-
Ternal verities will occupy my mind.
Is truth beauty? Or vice versa?
Will my health plan reimburse? A-
Gendas broader than the breadth of my behind
Will replace concerns with calories.
Global warming, teachers' salaries,
Kurds, and other urgent matters will prevent
Whining, wailing, and oi-veying
Over what, each day, I'm weighing.
Bodywise, I will be done with discontent.

In the meantime I feel pudgy
And the arrow will not budge, de-
Spite how lightly I try standing on my scale.
I had hoped to not begin this
Brand-new decade hooked on thinness
But it seems my weight obsession will prevail
Till I've finally banked my fires,
Till my vanity retires,
Till I've given up aspiring to size eight,
Till I scorn a foolproof diet.
Could I actually not try it?

Maybe *ninety* I won't care about my weight.

The Rest of It

I've done the who-am-I-and-where-am-I-going thing,
And the falling-in-love-and-isn't-it-wonderful thing,
And the married-with-kids-and-it's-not-always-wonderful thing,
And the having-it-all-or-whatever-the-hell-that-was thing.

I've done the midway-along-the-journey-of-my-life-I-woke-to-
    find-myself-lost-in-a-dark-wood-and-I-think-that-I'm-in-big-
    trouble-Dante's-*Inferno* thing,
And the meditation-and-medication-and-acupuncture-and-yoga-
    and-therapy thing,
And the more-or-less (though mostly less)-coming-to-terms-with-
    my-own-mortality thing,
And the I've-tripped-on-some-rocks-and-I've-bought-some-bad-
    stocks-and-I've-had-some-hard-knocks-but-I'm-still-here-
    Stephen-Sondheim-affirmational thing.
But the thing is, I'm still indeed here, and there appears to be
    more ahead,
And what am I planning to do with the rest of it?

Learning to rollerblade is not an option.
Nor are reading *Finnegan's Wake,*
Backpacking through Patagonia,
Acquiring a taste for shad roe,
Understanding quantum or any mechanics,
Or becoming the sort of woman who,
When told about an incredibly charming hotel in an exquisitely
    beautiful setting at an unbelievably low price, except the bath-
    room's down the hall,
Would ever, in a million years, want to go there.

Nonetheless, as I head toward
The packing-in-tennis-for-something-slower-
    like-golf thing,
And the isn't-it-time-to-sell-the-house-and-
    move-to-a-place-that-doesn't-have-all-these-
    stairs thing,
And the being-offered-a-seat-on-the-bus-by-a-woman-
    who-can't be-that-much-younger-than-I thing,
I will be learning to bake a nice olive bread,
Working on fixing the world,
Teaching my grandchildren how to play Monopoly,
Getting a second hole pierced in my left ear,
And trying, before I reach the maybe-I-ought-
    to-reconsider-those-arguments-on-behalf-
    of-an-afterlife thing,
To do my very best with the rest of it.

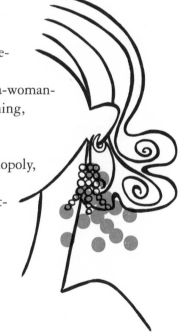